Love, Death, Sleep & Dreams

By

Ben Dunsky

AOS Publishing, 2025

ISBN: 978-1-990496-97-4
Cover Design: Nedjma Ziarati
Visit AOS Publishing's website:
www.aospublishing.com

À ma grand-mère,
Dont le doux sourire alimente
l'ascension du soleil levant

~

Introduction & Acknowledgments

This book is the product of years spent writing, thus its evolution
from pre-COVID to the present can be seen in every word.
Each poem represents moments of growth, reflection and
exploration.
My journey to complete this has been as rewarding as the final
product.

Whether you are a poetry lover or entirely unfamiliar with it, I
invite you to set aside any preconceived notions about what poetry
is 'supposed' to be.
This isn't just about understanding—it's about experiencing.
Poetry offers a sensory adventure, a momentary respite from daily
life and an opportunity to immerse yourself in a unique auditory
and visual experience.
Each word is a brushstroke, capable of evoking a feeling, a
memory, or an image that sparks your imagination.

So,
I must extend a huge thank you to everyone:
who has supported me in my pursuits as a writer,
who listened to endless drafts and edits,
who shared in my excitement and encouraged me through
moments of doubt,
to everyone who has gotten involved and encouraged my creative
arts collective - ABC,
to AOS Publishing for their friendly collaborative spirit,
to the city of Montreal and all artists within who are trying to
make it,
to Vietnam and Argentina and the people who inspired me on my
travels,
to the gentlemen of KA,
to my family and friends for always believing in me,
And lastly to the natural world for continually inspiring me with its
inconceivably complicated grace.

Thank you!

TABLE OF CONTENTS

Poems

October in Montreal

During those last days of warmth
when we can feel
both subtly cold afternoons
and the memory of
winter threatening us

we all go out
in t-shirts
as if to say,
No,
It will be warm forever

Am Cầu

I left you on an island
with seclusion
but house enough
after months of hosting you at mine
and even longer in my body

I spat you out over the crashing waves
after you had hollowed me to completion

So you,
parasitic in nature and action,
can live there now,
and under the November summer sun,
I say, Adieu!

Last day

Today was the last day in the blue forest,
my last day scraping beams
of orange light
from between the wide
purple and turquoise leaves
that catch-and-hold
little ponds of rainwater on their brow.
It was my last with the singing grubs and the whistling apes,
my last feeling the porous moss between my
now heavily-calloused toes.
It was my last clear,
star-filled evening,
standing under the wheeling heavens,
spinning the syllables of your name
around on my tongue
like hard candy
or arsenic

Because tomorrow is the day
I finally force you out,
and you'll poison the roots and
the pearls that hang from the branches.
You'll burn the canopy and choke the sky
with silver plumes of black smoke.
The water will taste metallic
in place of
Its crystal rum perfume,
and the animals will wretch
sour black dough from their chests.

You call yourself the vengeance
of an ancient anger
or Earth's icy retribution,
but I see your naked skin
pale in the gagged moonlight
gasping for a castaway glance.
I see your blued skin,
broken soul,
and the tar that tips out
from the cauldron behind your teeth
over your perfect lips
and onto the world
you want so badly to kill

Sometimes flying

That same sound
That ties this apartment
To my memories
Strikes again,
Reminding me of when it was full
And empty,
Reminding me of happiness
And loss,
Reminding me of the passage of time
And the futility of the moment
And the screaming into pillows
And cork marks in the ceiling from bottles of cheap champagne
And missing friends
And a haze over the plants that dutifully guard my front
window

It's three years in this one now
So many seconds I can barely remember.
This is an earnest and most well-intentioned nest,
Home of carnage
And birth
And fleeting warmth
And sometimes,
In my luckiest moments,
Flying

Toothless incantation

Stone brick, Mossbane root
Circlesmith laughing meadsick
Sultry hollow-horn drank through
Choking at the middle
And end of each toothless incantation

Hastily headlong into the human hive
Heavy sights are heaped
Onto my cross-rotten eyes
That look through the scrying flower,
One that bulbs and vibes
Covered in the sweat
Cast from cloud above
Curse-calling the antelope that saved you
Babed and wrecked
On crocodile river
That day you were drenched and lifted
To a life
That lingered ever so slightly

And so now that it was
Somewhat of a specialty,
Linger I did,
Deeper into the tangled mat
Of screams and sellers,
And so lost did I become
In steam and violence
That the moment was
Impossible to surmount

Suddenly caught by my naked indiscretion
And red-hot pride,
I fathomed that I had flown into a great cage
Marked by mighty bars
That shined dull with callous indifference

So there I was
All at once cellmate with the great heart that sings evil truth
In a slippery and swan song tone.
It tells me of memories gone and prophecies to come;
It played gold-caped and coated lies for all of us to eat.

But far worse was the fate of the observer,
For once the blood-beater
Was done brooding in backward lip,
It dumped you into some reposit basin
To toil amid the bones and stripped refuse
Trapped thus
Listening until thoughts are gradually replaced
With the chorus of vicious buzzing
From above

Hammer

When we walked
On that final night
Not a word or smile
Between the two of us,
I realized
That you had never really been there

You were never here

And all at once,
As you vanished from view,
You shifted back into a stranger

How will I know

How will I know
If I'm doing it right,
If not for a contrasting experience,
If not for withdrawing Excalibur
Out darkest Wednesday
Moment or thought?

How will I know when it is time for me?
When it's no longer time for you?
When whistling wind
Slows its singing and casts
Beams of sun's song chorus
Onto a spun, weblocked day?

How will I know
When the brain rot
Has set in too deep?
Must I surrender more hourglass sand?
Or will dreamswitch shock me to my senses,
Gasping breathlessly with delirium
In the chirpless four am grey?

How will I know if I'm doing it right
If I'm so blighted by the present moment
So wiped clean with the early week's steel wool
What must I do
If my palace
Feels more like a glue trap
Than home's necessary and
Needed embrace?

The only new words left are tucked away,
Hidden in books unopened or
Routinely undesired
Like the blue heron at the far side of the lake,
Silently witnessed but undisturbed

So let then the day be tied up with lustre,
Uncommon gems, and greenstalk

Let then the stories of imagination
Spill from panopticon head;
Let them flow forth
With the aggression of a protective mother
And drown the countryside
With only the violence
That true creativity whispers about the world

Tongue twister beginning

The door-floor lawyer
Shaded and glued
Aimed to settle the score,
Shrimping and shrinking
Around the yellow pen
Once more

He stuck and sprinkled
Bits of deformed dough
Onto griffoned and gritted
Cutting cloth
Made milky
By the rinsed resign recycling
Raucous and raging
Behind red intent and iron

Stansmithed soupstock sours
In the oven of our orbed
Outlook monastery—
And you bet your ass we orbited
Oddly in the Alps that afternoon
Axeled and audited,
But naked and greedy for more of you

And you've,
Unyielding and aggressively,
Caused the recent uprisings
In my dreams,
Drunk and daylit

In the bed that sleeps
Me most of the time.
On good nights,
Noble and rare though they are,
Mothersquiled and mayhemtorn,
Misty and frozen for more than half the year,
We used to hide under there
And share breath;
All the layers of the earth were on top of us
Like a weighted promise we both hated
And broke immediately

Paradox

You have no idea how easy life could be
Because of how hard it seems

Why was cutting butter a labour,
When shattering the moon is a right?

Everything was always true
Or false,
But at least
With a convincing sheen of truth
In the world of perfect
That has never existed

EchoMetaphor

Purple dress maiden
Winding cobbled stairs—
The grass in the back fields is only cut
Twice a year.
It laps like water at our ankles,
Like warm hide-and-seek shallows,
Thick thrushes to hide in

In the green sea
Only gold birds stand white against the sky,
Hanging motionless as if never moved

Black-flecked beaks point the same way
As pearl ivory and oak bow
While crisp sails snap and crack in the salty air

Far below
In ripping-hot cavern
Encased within the Earth,
Neutral chaos churns in cherry brine.
Heat
Like pungent aura
Calling nostalgic chords of yore
In the dim glow

Back when the Phoenix first winked its eye
At the distant crust of a faraway universe,
It foretold the fated impact of space dust
Upon the beaches of ancient ice ages,
Entombed until unearthed
A knot tying the galaxies together.

That's why they call it a diamond

Leatherworker

Miasma minded
cutting leather in my
white-hot sunroom

Beads of water tumbling heavily
down the shimmering windows
clearframing stroller dogs
gasping in dusty air

At dusk
the sulphur moment plays
on reems of wax reels,
catapulting characters through your old projector
onto the glass.
They speak in the voice of God,
and it booms relentless and sure-tongued
over the speakers of the town's most secular nightclub
half-full of serpent-slithered clientele,
who kissed the words into our minds
until we were leather workers,
pleased and fat and sated in our sunlit fantasies

At night
we know some truth has sprung up,
washed free from shallow burial

We hear acid spill
from the corner of the Grand illusion

The sunroom has a burnt-out light bulb

The ruby grapefruit spills pearls of juice
onto that golden carpet
among sunbeams
and small strips of leather

Park Laf

The trees crawled up from the ground as though they were
escaping from it

Pale white-and-black striped bark,
like some exalted prisoner
finally free from
the clutches of an infamous,
reclusive jailor,
far below the grass

In the shifting air,
Maple Longbranch swaying
reads sundesperate
and delirious,
as their green leaves
reach curiously
for the sun

On Wednesday

On Wednesday
I split my oak door
and turned it into a canoe
so I could paddle the river
of thoughts—

Thoughts that flowed
and bubbled
and churned
from the spout of
iron teapot
in which
was the black tea
only the emperor drank

He sipped in pensive daze,
and in those small moments he
pondered the scattered clouds
in the sun's blue reflection

Sundress summer flyby

Sundress summer flies by
Just as birds into glass,
The seasons cycle

Like dusk to dawn

Steadily upward
Rolls the sun
To bake the clay
And I,
Like some
Confused sculptor,
Position myself
Between them
As if it were my
Responsibility to
Stop the Earth from splitting
In two

When time loses its meaning

When time loses its meaning
On any sprawling plain
The peaks of nearby mountains
Will bend to greet you without a sound

I will brush against that sensation
To get us started

When I am gutless
And strung up,
Whipped and gored
For passing fancy,
The trees will breathe your name
As I find the strength to persevere
And die in your distant company
At sunset

When the sun has become
A figment of a memory
I will drift into sleep's embrace
In a backyard pool,
Or deep in some underwater ruin,
In which I'll search
For ancient markings
That tell of a love that
Tirelessly circles the globe,
Ripping out the dead trees
And blowing the arctic wind
That cyclones the stacked refuse
On grey street corners.

So now
When remembering
In a final moment
As I board the ferry
Over blacklake,
I imagine a simple lunch
Where I'll say something
That chimes like a bell
Resonating with another,
And we'll both know
That we're awake

Sheetsong

He longs to leave an impression
without complexity;
he is shallow,
dense, and immature,

So he'll lie stubbornly abreast,
clasped to her as a boy,
or a husband,
and listen to her breaths
between words,
to the air in her chest
as it rises and sinks

When she adjusts her body
static cling makes tundra wind
in sliding sheets

I will memorize the extremities
of that moment.
The gravity of silence with you
feels like ocean weight

I pray to stay
in that limbo
until you dig through the world
and look through
the filthy glass kaleidoscope
that catches me
emerging from the Earth,
searching for your eyes

Tightscarf Sleepslumber

The first time I lost sleep I struggled to find it;
I checked its cage
To find steel bars,
Tooth-marked and gnawed
In the shape of a
Violent and panicked escape

So I set about searching
The wide plains
In all their furious winds
To find it

I pulled on my boots
And rushed to button my coat
As the clouds threatened with a mighty rain

I tied my scarf tight.

When first over the barricade,
my feet touched the wet earth.
I felt the plates below tremble
As if the seam of reality was fraying,
Sucking asteroids out of space,
Calling to Hades
And begging his influence hence

I began to search for a mountain
That could save me
from the coming floods,
One that could stand unmoved against

The waters or the magma,
Whatever it was that seemed fated
To wipe the green from the Earth

When the mountain was near,
Thousands of birds tore up the sky,
Stabbing at the grey clouds
Scattering out of formation
Like broken glass,
And they screamed past me
Like the night siren
Like the crash of a distant but ferocious wave
Like good news in the mail

When I finally capped the mountain,
And the sky hung low,
It scraped against my head

I had found my escaped beast.
I knelt near its shivering torso
And wrapped my arms around it,
As if to comfort my own child,
When pale beams of yellow and blue
Shot from its body and,
From a now quickly-plummeting sky,
Called me into a dream

But this was one from which I would never wake.

Warm earth

I take water from the Earth
I suck its meats from quivering bone
I shave crystal lens
And bend light to my purpose
I scrawl my story
On rock and parchment

Though imbued
With free will and power,
I revel in apathy
I piss into a bowl

—Oh, whispered tongue
And paper trade.
Oh, spacecraft
And millions
Of bent lenses—

Because imbued
With strength and evil,
My mark on this Earth
Is not cheap
But I'll spare myself
The responsibility
Through deities
Of my own creation

I'll drink from the
Most secret River
And sharpen my teeth
On a tree I've felled,
Or a stone

I'll lie on the warm earth,
And with white eye turned
Now mostly black,
Stare into the heavens,
Scanning
For what to eat next

Bulgebreak

I will look for you

I'll start in the grassy fen,
Then to land's end
Through bubbling tar pits
And forgotten wood.
I'll ride a greybeard
Straight out of my chin
Looking for you

All at once
Some tableau transfixes me,
And in one of life's purely natural moments
Allures me out of my search

~

The black loons jut out
Of soft-lit marshy shallows
Where the land is unsure of itself,
Sloppy and wet,
Where it bulges and breaks
Into the summer waves,
Crashing against the fading day
Butterflynetting what is now
Only a colourful memory.

It's a universal celebration,
A visible ebb and flow latticework

When suddenly,
In some random future second
When I'm reminded of my search,
The moment bursts
And bleeds out against the sky

Solar Cessation

Plunge,
Plunge deep into the well
And trudge through the viscous mire
That's been cast there
From unfamiliar faces

Step on antlers and tusks
And climb to the red light—
One that lays your
Body bare beneath the blaze,
One that strips you beyond,
Past the point of understanding,
Until vulnerable
Is just a word
With a no longer fathomable definition,
Until you yearn for the rotten well
In all its putrid muck and
Convalescent darkness,

But cast yourself still
Onto cracked rock,
Black-blue obsidian ballast
Casting horrible shadows over the
Turmoil of the day,
Over the tormented blood,
Thrust out from deep below
Where the unthinkable sleeps

And the air is too lame with salt
Too salty for dreams or
Feverish love,
Too muggy to see
How lost to you is time.
For in your scarlet haze, you realize
How nearly you've approached
The blistering boil
That glistens only in apocalypse,
In wicked eclipse,
The tumult that makes crows fly rampant
And with recklessness
Enough that wild smiles are visible behind beaks
In many a glazed and glossy sideways eye.

So it is true
That chaos coats
Every inch
Of this blighted brae,
This turgid landscape
That bleats and moans
Into the unending swirl
That gives seed to the red trees
That offer protection from no light.
For they are burnt, broken and bent
Into odd shapes
That pull the skin back
In a magnetising effect

And it is true that this journey has been wretched and necessary
So you, clamouring up steep cliff face
In an effort to get away,

In your castaway nakedness
Before sour terrain marks your fallibility
And lack of foresight,
You will know Hell and Earth collided
Into one land
That pricks the foot with each step,
That scratches at eyes and pulls at the
Nails and teeth,
An unending nightmare
Worn like a brand
Deep inside your mind

Coal Sapling

Midway down the mountain
there is a secret glade
with tightly-packed
pine and spruce
poking out of the snow.
When the wind picks up
they sway a bit,
as if to ask you to dance.
I can see them now
with a knotted smile
barked out into a time
that I struggle to remember,
one uprooted from memory.

This is my perfect forest.
The trees are resolute and strong.
They speak in earthy tones
that I might hear
if I sit long enough to listen.
Maybe then I could finally learn
of their secret truths.

Not long after that,
the mountain was moved.
The land under
tilled and seeded.
The fields were fully threshed
and cities built
from a viscous grey mix.

The black smoke from chimneys
sprays coal ash into the throats of children
so that they cannot
whisper any truths.
It was as if they had collectively hoisted
a false golden idol
and decided that it was God.

I can see
from my window,
the parade of idolatry.
The buzzing from the crowd
—unnerving—
like the sound of some frightened nest
or a modern threat you cannot grasp.
I've seen them defend their reality
with steadfast, self-justified violence.
I could try now,
through my coal lung,
to recall the glade
and all that white snow,

before sour blood
poisoned the harbour water
that is sucked up
In rueful silence,
before the fog stank of rot,
fog that sustains fractured lives that spill tar from their hearts
in place of love.
Before the sky was darkened.

Before a thin film coated every surface with a
monochromatic grease.

I can picture it while I pace around this den that soaks itself in
lamplight, the trees that throw back their heads reaching for
celestial peace.
But when I dream,
I am pulled somewhere altogether worse.
Into a tangible feeling
that it will never snow again.

A long day; a long life

A public display around the yard
with tulips abounding

A quiet look in the
underground room
with dust settled on the urns

A long laugh at the back of a bar
where your head rolls around
and looks at nothing in particular

A dress hiked up and
legs splashing in the
mirror clear brook—
eyes follow toes,
each step is taken carefully

A longpull
of something you rolled yourself
in a grey den

And a fleeting thought
of the hours and hours
and hours
gone by

~

And still
a most brilliant love
for friends and food
for watching the building burn

And still
a tremendous respect
for discipline
and bravery
for those who hear the meaning
or intention
behind words

So leave the curtains drawn
in the hued dusk
that reads to you in
pinks, purples, and blues

And dream deeply
as if it were an earnest prayer
asking to be awoken by
another sun

Fleeting Breeze or A Home Long Since Visited

Can love be affixed to a neck?
Like a golden promise whispered along skin,

like a dream that lives on a warm shore—
under some foreign constellation—
that gazes up and feels an invisible weight.

I've never understood what's at stake,
what could have possibly been lost.

When was it that something
that was so hard fought
could drift down a river
or across the ocean
into a dicey afternoon
of temperate climate and middling light.
Who could have known
to pray
for that blue moon?

(It's all gone like it never happened—
in a spray—
like some migration
that bows its head and makes itself known
and I,
remembering that warm shore
under some foreign constellation
will look to the waves
or the waning moon
for an answer.)

Pressed Papyrus is a Nightmare Worth Having

There are sunbeams,
And there are days where I fear the page,
Where the street corner feels far,
When the house arrest feels mandatory

And there are other days where the red reminds me of plump
fruit
Or youthful ambition,
But only after you've first seen blood
At the tip of your thumb
Leaking out of a scrape.
Only after the blue you describe
Sinks deeper than the ocean
With all its unknown trenches
And eats at the edge of the sky
So it can be rolled around in an open palm
While curious eyes take apart the strings of the moment.

Now,
There are whole months comprised of Sundays and Monday
mornings
There are weeks where washing the smoke out of your brain
feels like a full-time job.
But I'll still find time to love,
Like the way you love a field where no one can find you,
When what grows there is inconsequential,
But it's definitely barley,
Or fiddlehead ferns.

So when the water tells you of a season change
By making it too cold to swim,
Or too ominous,
Remember the warmth of the red
And the profundity of the blue,
And write until spring comes to kiss you on the head.

The Book you Buy

To love another
it must be a full love,
or else it is a love of reluctance.
To desire them
is to spend weeks underground
hungry for piercing light.
To nourish them
you must find the oldest tree
packed tightly with deep knots,
or the toughest fish
with broad scales that reflect the midday gleam,
and learn their secrets
of longevity
and gravitas.
Learn of soft truths
that blanket the Earth
in all seasons—
ones that make themselves known
in barely a
dulcet whisper.

To love another
you must give up reason
and so to give up what you know.
Trust in a bond formed fresh
like molten iron meeting
quenching oil.
Step out into midnight
and believe in it.

Let its soft darkness swirl around your legs
and remember faith
as though it were an anthem
committed to memory but long since sung
on your usual walk
down by the river.

The stillness of the moment is balanced,
weighed in marble arms,
like some great Athenian statue
that regards you from the clouds
or some mountain's peak
and sees only parts of herself.
Feel greed, torment, and envy
and still know grace, and tranquillity,
because she teaches you
out in the rain with a look,
or under the blankets
with a sound.

To love another
you must feel it
in every fibre,
every pore
—make it natural

make it mass—
let it run free
like no other thought.
Give it the rights to your soul
and sign in an ink you didn't know you had.

She's Penicillin

Now that the lamplight is fading
And the gold scarf of youth is fraying
But still familiar,
She preaches without a word.

Now that the quest is near won
And the dragon is a face
Among faces,
She will ride behind you,
And her hands
Will slide along your body.

Now that the desert and the coast have been mapped,
-After listening to the fierce wind that carries oven heat-
We'll walk from dune to rocky shoal
And mark the teeming life of the estuaries
To page and to memory.
She'll bend over the rocks and peer into the water.
I cannot fathom her, so while stunned
The seafoam will roll along the sand and kiss
My pant legs
As a reminder.

Now that the dark star has been grasped
In a palm
Or a newscast
And there is no reason
To venture out
Into frozen waste,

She will look at you from bed while
You pace about the room,
Searching for where sleep could be hidden.
And when the golden chariot bursts
from the opal clouds on that
Brilliant ruby day and dances in the amethyst sky,
My eyes will burn like amber.
And though I will finally understand,
I'll still look back to see if you're coming, too.

The First Pages of Ash

Breathe me a song of fire
So I can dance in its light
In the late evening

Sing loud so the forest
Whispers for furry ears to stay away
While embers snap and claw
In their own tongue

Join me,
And we will pound our feet black
In the settled ash

Take my hand
And slide into my life
Like cutting glass
Or the first thoughts of
Feverish, terrifying love
That leaves you gutless
—(As foreign reflection of the boy
You had grown out of,
Vulnerable and curious)---
Wasted on the rocks
Below claimed cliff
Under some red banner
That you are now oathsworn to,
In the name of love,
In her name

Sleep with me
And try at the thoughts
That call to the great beyond
That dip their paddle into black lake.

And finally,
Watch the white deer dance in trampled foliage
Breathe in a pocketed moment dated from childhood,
Talk of great love with shining eyes,
And be warm together near the fire.

My Code

My code is one
Only I know

I'll find it sometimes
When I clear away
Dirt and dust,
Or hear it at the
End of a sentence
As if the words
Were imbued
With the power
And secrecy of candlelight

I'll smell it
Leering out of
Hazy kitchens
With uneven footing

In the lamplight dotted
Summer air
I can finally hear it!
Like I have so many times before,
Echoing off the walls

There you are,
Singing carelessly
In the bathtub
And with a smile, you'll say,
"You're asking me to do something I could never do."

Time is a Gas

In the middle of the room was the vessel.
Chained,
bound there, by gold-clasp.
In books with new pages of ash,
I learn this vessel is impenetrable.
How then did my mother
give brass keys with dying breath
that fit snug in the impossible locks?
Must I fracture and dislocate
bones and joints
to slide past the chains and traps?
Do I remember these halls from before?
From when I walked down
these obsidian steps,
for what was maybe an hour
or a month
or a year.
Was it in a dream?
Suppose I were to recount
what my mind calls memories,
what shining spoils would I gather in my beak
from shallow fishing?
Would I remember this vessel from before?
It has a dazzling figure,
a pearled basin with red carvings.
It glows in the mildewed light, gold-tucked and bent,
and jade stone abounding.
The fires of the Earth cast gold light *déja-vu*.

I have been here before, I have picked those locks
and contorted through the chains
I have willed my hand to the rim, to the lip, and peered inside.
And that glance lasted for eternity,
for one true unending moment.
And it's beautiful,
and it might be perfect.
If only I could find a way to think in curses.
For a time I allow these thoughts to overtake me and
to drive me to the lip. There, peering over the rim,
the colours are grey and muted in the mist,
dulled by their post, copper-worn, leathered.
And such is the case with life from time to time.
Compelled up black rock steps with slippery lesson in hand,
I feel as though I know I will be back. Like the assuredness
and inevitability of your favourite spot on an old couch.
"This is my vessel," I whisper to nobody.
Skating up stairs of vanishing recollection,
how did I get here?
The answer is already fading into last week
When an eagle dropped a flight feather
And there was nothing left for it to land on.